A LEAP OF (INTER)FAITH

FINDING TREASURES THROUGH SHARED PRACTICE

AMBER MATTINGLEY

AND

LISA ANTONIOTTI (NGAWANG PEMA)

Topical Line Drives, Volume 46

Energion Publications
Gonzalez, Florida
2022

ISBN: 978-1-63199-802-7
eISBN: 978-1-63199-803-4

Energion Publications
PO Box 841
Gonzalez, FL 32560
https://energion.com
pubs@energion.com

TABLE OF CONTENTS

A special thank you to Domo Geshe Rinpoche without whose teaching this project and subsequent study would not be possible.

Introduction

(Amber)

My first class at Claremont School of Theology met on a stage and the chairs were set up in a large circle. As I looked around a room with many smiling faces, Pema's smile stood out from the crowd. I noticed that she was different from the other students, yet there was a heartfelt quality that drew me towards Pema. I've experienced this before with a few individuals and found that when I follow this instinct, I recognize a kindred spirit. In digging a little deeper, I realized that I am oriented towards those who are different from the group, desiring to offer friendship, respect, and inclusion. My experience of being the "Other" softens my heart towards those who might feel the same way. So when I entered the doctoral program at Claremont School of Theology in 2017, I immediately noticed Pema.

In our third year together, I took a class called Multi-Religious Contemplative Capacities for Engaged Compassion. I was interested in this class because it gave me the opportunity to engage spiritual practices from a variety of religious traditions. The final project intrigued me the most. The instructions directed me to find a person from a religious tradition that is different than mine and to ask them to teach me a practice. Pema immediately came to my mind. My request was not just for her to teach me any practice, but one that felt dear to her heart. My intention was to better understand a practice that was heartful because I felt our emerging friendship was about a deeper connection than what we initially considered.

SHARED PRACTICE

(Pema)

When I first met Amber, I thought she was a conservative Southern Christian. As a Buddhist, I was unsure if I should speak with her because I felt she may not want to speak with me. But I do not always believe the first thing that I think. Instead, I chose to get to know her. We met on the first day of our doctoral program at the Methodist founded Claremont School of Theology (CST), where there seemed to be a more diverse group of clergy than usual. Among a cohort of about 40, there were Pentecostals, Seventh Day Adventists, Episcopalians, Methodists, Baptists, Disciples, Coptic Christians, Lutherans, and Unitarian Universalists. Surprisingly, there were as many women as men. Yet as a Buddhist in flowing maroon robes, I still appeared very different. Our mutual curiosity led Amber and I to quickly become friends.

In my third-year project, I wanted to better understand modern Christian spirituality. I chose to interview Amber regarding her spiritual history and her beliefs in God and Jesus. I asked about her spiritual practices and experience before we met, and about defining moments in her spiritual history. It was particularly interesting for me because Amber has practiced or been exposed to so many different traditions within Christianity.

Based on my experience in Buddhism, I wonder about the depth at which Christianity is generally practiced, even among the clergy. I have asked myself what would happen if a Christian practitioner had access to some of the practices I know, which have radically deepened my sense of spirituality and embodiment. Are they available in some parts of Christianity? If practiced, would Christians learn something new (or recover something lost)? Would those practices enliven their sense of spirituality and give them further access to Christian wisdom? I've also wondered if perhaps more profound spiritual methods (mechanisms of practice) can apply across the traditions, divorced from their outer cultural form.

These questions were on my mind as we prepared to share a spiritual practice. These questions boiled down to three lines of inquiry in our projects. What insights would be gained by sharing the Buddhist version of the purification and increase Practice[1] with a Christian? Would it move Amber to a deeper heartfeltness and deeper understanding of spirituality in her own faith tradition? Could the mechanism of practice move from Buddhism to Christianity so that Amber could continue to practice this meditation in her own tradition?

1 See "The Mediation" p. 15.

4

About Pema

(Amber)

Pema grew up as an only child. Her parents divorced when she was two. Pema lived with her mother, and they struggled financially until she was seven. When Pema was in second grade, she moved from the north where she attended an academically rigorous Catholic school to living in the south and attending a public school that was not academically challenging for her. Pema reported, "Since I was one year ahead in some of my classes, I spent half my day with the academically accelerated students and half of my day in classes with students who were not accelerated. I was also a "Yankee" who lived on the border between the Black farmers and the White farmers."[2] During this time Pema befriended a Black girl from her school and was treated with hospitality by her Black neighbors even though White people were not typically welcomed. When the girls turned 16, they drifted apart because their friendship was not socially permitted.

When Pema entered college, she attended an affluent school where many of the girls dreamed of being mothers and housewives, but Pema dreamed of becoming a scientist. Secretly, she was also interested in helping people make their dreams come true. Pema reports that she did not know how to do this exactly, but this became the direction of her vocation. Pema had a career in the business world and then pursued a Master's degree in Education. The emphasis of this degree was in adult education and counseling therapy. In 2017, Pema entered the Doctor of Ministry Program at Claremont School of Theology. The program focuses on spiritual renewal, contemplative practice, and strategic leadership.

Pema's journey to becoming a monastic-ordained Tibetan Buddhist touches many different religious traditions along the way. While growing up, Pema's mother was atheist and her father was nominally Catholic. Pema grew up going to Catholic school, but when they moved to the south, she did not have a Catholic church nearby. This change began a period of searching that lead her to

---

2 Lisa Antoniotti. "A Stranger in a Strange Land: The Healing Effects of Purification and Increase Meditation, Spiritual Friendship, And Life on The Fringe." (Doctoral Project. Claremont School of Theology, 2020).

connect to Native American Shamanism, New Age spiritualities, and Unitarian Universalists. It wasn't until she attended a Buddhist teaching in her mid 20's that she felt at home. Pema heard the Four Noble Truths explained as a path to help people live their dream of being happy and healthy. At last, Pema had found a religious home.

Currently, Pema teaches in a variety of capacities. She co-founded and teaches at Joyful Path Meditation and Healing Center. The center has a mission to facilitate individual and community transformation through meditation instruction, complementary healing services, and Dharma service. She uses her background as a yoga therapist in her work as a mental health clinician. She also works as a hospital chaplain and has enjoyed the opportunity of teaching on a variety of health and wellness topics. When Pema taught Amber the Buddhist meditation practice and saw the results, creating a larger project to study the effects of the practice became the focus of Pema's dissertation at CST.

About Amber
(Pema)

Amber is a 42-year-old ordained American Baptist. She was married in 2001 and is a mother of two. Born in Victoria, Texas, she spent most of her childhood there, although she and her family spent a year in California and a year in Virginia while she was growing up. Amber is the oldest child of five siblings. Amber reports her early years were filled with challenges and some specific traumatic events, but there were also times of joy. In response to a family member's struggle with alcoholism, Amber became a secondary parental figure to her siblings. She always felt called to ministry. In junior high, an Elder in her Methodist church told her that she had a ministry of healing in her future.

Amber enjoyed and excelled at the academic aspects of school. In high school she was the quintessentially popular cheerleader being named Homecoming Queen as a senior, except she participated in all of the social cliques in the school and would not confine herself to a single clique. Although there was not a lot of diversity where she lived, she was the person who always sought out the outsider. For example, "In Catholic school we had one Muslim student whose family originated from Pakistan, and I was the only person who was allowed to come to her home for a play date. I found myself in these interesting situations like going to an expensive preparatory high school where I befriended students who lived on the other side of town – these experiences kept my heart a little soft and the space more open…"[3] This theme carries through in Amber's worldview today.

Amber was ordained in the American Baptist church in 2000, and her husband is also ordained. In 2005, they were called to a Disciples church, where they immediately connected to the theology and mission of this denomination. Amber received a call in 2015 to be the Associate Pastor at the same church where her spouse was the Lead Pastor. The ministry experience began with creativity and depth and ended two years later with devastating results for both the church and Amber. Amber felt unfairly targeted by a group within the church when she implemented plans that the

---

3 Mattingly. "Interview."

church had agreed to in the interview process. The church parking lot gossip undermined her leadership. Amber reports that she tried to be herself at the beginning of her call, then tried to be who they wanted her to be, and both tries failed to connect to this group. Amber said, "I felt like God had created me with a particular set of skills, called me to this church, and then abandoned me for the wolves to feast upon." In 2017, Amber started the Doctor of Ministry program at CST after ending this difficult pastor-couple assignment, though her husband remained at that church. After much consideration, in 2019, Amber initiated the process of transferring her ordination to the Disciples. Amber then completed a pivotal Yoga teacher-training program before entering Claremont, which she characterizes as a very healing experience.

Amber entered Claremont with this aching wound from her past church experience. She questioned where her path would lead and what her next call might be. She has subsequently developed an innovative ministry for "people on the fringe," which she researched in her doctoral project. She offers an experience that has at its core the integration of Christian spirituality and Yoga (a system of spiritual formation that can be used in conjunction with most religions).

Working at the Fringe

(Pema)

Western culture seems to reinforce a sense of strangers as a kind of alien or Unknown Other who inhabit places beyond the borders of our own life. We often have a strong sense of separation and a sense of difference with these Unknown Others. They are often seen as less valuable than our friends and allies. But if we stop and think about it, we can look around and see that family and friends can quickly become strangers and even enemies. Strangers can become friends.

Buddhism proposes that the fundamental problem is that almost all of us are confused about overcoming suffering and creating lasting happiness. We all share a common hope of happiness/wellness and a common problem of confusion (or ignorance of how to create lasting happiness and wellness). Every "problem" I have heard seems to boil down to this common wish and challenge.

For me, Pema, this commonality dissolves the distance between myself and the Unknown Other, and we become what in Christian circles I sometimes call the "Sacred Other." The Sacred Other appears as a stranger, or Unknown Other, but upon further examination, we find the Sacred Other is as close and valuable as that which we hold most Sacred. When I describe the "Sacred Other," some of my Christian colleagues call to mind the parable of the Good Samaritan. Although I have not studied this parable in depth, I might say that in this parable Jesus is using an extreme example to show that our neighbors are all those who are suffering. But in addition, the Sacred Other is an intimate other because we hold them valuable and sacred, and so they are held close in our hearts. In Tibetan Buddhism, "All Sentient Beings" are equally dear and worthy of our compassion, and also worthy to be free of suffering and to have lasting happiness. To me, the "Sacred Other" is a representative, standing in the front of a line comprised of All Sentient Beings, worthy of this same compassion and freedom.

Moving to the fringe might be a way to serve others, especially the lonely and abandoned beings who often inhabit that space. More importantly, maybe the fringe is one place where the boundaries between ourselves and the Unknown Other more easily dissolve. Or maybe when we have the chance to offer hospitality at the fringe, we simply realize that there is no border at all.

In this way, encountering strangers – the Unknown Others that appear in daily life – was the start of a profoundly transformative journey with Amber that gave rise to new avenues of research. When Amber engaged in the practice, she reported positive spiritual, mental, and emotional changes. She also reported physical healing effects. A year of daily practice combined with ongoing interfaith dialogue became the impetus for us to become co-researchers, along with my spiritual mentor, in a subsequent exploratory research study. Our questions evolved to the following: "Could the mechanism of a specific purification and increase practice of Tibetan Buddhism help move practitioners of the Buddhist and Christian traditions into a new spiritual depth, bringing a more profound understanding and experience of wellness and a more fully embodied experience of their spirituality? What effects are attributable to the practice of purification and increase?"

Although we had engaged in spiritual practice for years, the wealth of information in the results of the study was unanticipated. The results echoed Amber's breadth and depth of experience and led us to deep insights about how a practice like this might lead to spiritual growth for both Christians and Buddhists. There are many ways that people from differing faith traditions come together in service to the world. The effect is building relationships across traditions based on a common mission of compassion. What this study suggests is that there is potential for spiritual growth through shared practices.

We were not strongly focused on Buddhist-Christian theology. However, we realized that our experience included a growing interfaith relationship that gave insights into one way that we can deeply and intimately come to love our neighbor. It is not through remaining at the borders of our traditions, but it is through the willingness to cross over to visit the spiritual home of the Other, that we have gained these insights. While there are many insights from our projects and study, in this work we hope to share the gifts of the interfaith experience, the power of this practice, and the story of our journey to very close Spiritual Friends.

Our Traditions

(Amber)

I, Amber, grew up connected with many denominations (Methodist, non-denominational, Episcopal, Catholic, Baptist, American Baptist, and Disciples of Christ). I appreciate the spectrum of beliefs and practices found within Christianity. My foundation is that all people are created in God's image as found in Genesis 1:27. Jesus observed how labels of holy/unholy, sacred/secular, saved/unsaved created divisions between people. I see Jesus modeling *radical inclusion* by inviting people to see differently, trusting that if they accepted the invitation then their behavior would reflect their new way of seeing.[4] He offered "an alternative vision of the human community"[5] by inviting outcasts, sinners, and saints into table fellowship. Jesus showed us that God never created these divisions because God is love.

If the very essence of God is love, then the fruit of following Jesus would first be to love God with all of our heart, mind, and spirit and to love our neighbor as ourselves as found in Luke 10:27. John 13:35 says, "By this everyone will know that you are my disciples, if you have love for one another" and Matthew 5:44 adds, "But I say to you, Love your enemies and pray for those who persecute you so that you may be children of your father in heaven." This love is within each of us, but we must *become aware* of our innately divine nature and find practices that invite us to continue to say yes to fully express our likeness of God in the world.

To my way of thinking, Jesus came to earth to show what it would look like to be in total union with God and that the power to be in total union with God is available to all. The incarnation did not just happen once at the birth of Jesus but is continuing to happen in each of our lives as we align ourselves with Jesus' teaching and follow him in compassionate action.[6] Jesus said in John 15:4, "Abide in me as I abide in you. Just as the branch cannot bear fruit by itself unless it abides in the vine, neither can you unless

---

4 Huston Smith, *The World's Religions* (New York: Harper One, 1991), 325.
5 Ibid, 325.
6 Phillip Novak, *The World's Wisdom: Sacred Texts of the World's Religions* (New York: Harper One, 1994), 270.

you abide in me." In these words, he is using intimate words of incarnation. The image of the vine and the branch being sustained by the same nourishment and encouraged to grow through the same light source moves beyond a sense of physical closeness to an embodied experience. As a Christian, I might say, "May I embody more of the qualities of Jesus every day."

Within Buddhism there are many branches. Pema is an ordained Tibetan Buddhist, a branch that is divided into four major schools. Within each school there are lineages, which we might think of as like a "Protestant denomination." A lineage holder is a "saintly being" present in every generation, the student of the previous lineage master. They are acknowledged to hold the same realizations as the original teacher. "Great emphasis is placed on the sense of continuity that comes from a lineage of the unbroken transmission of a practice that has been kept without degeneration."[7] Each student can trace from their generation's teacher all the way back to the Buddha in an unbroken series.

Pema embraces the foundational teaching of the Four Noble Truths as one of the great treasures of her tradition.

> The First Noble Truth is that everyone suffers. The Second is that there is a cause for this suffering. The cause of our suffering is sometimes described as inappropriate craving, but is probably best described as ignorance or confusion. This confusion we all experience naturally clouds our view and interferes with our virtues and our wisdom, obscuring them and creating more difficult obstacles in our spiritual lives. The Third is that there is a way to end our suffering, and The Fourth describes the method or the "prescription" given by the Buddha to end our experience of suffering, which is called the Noble Eightfold Path. The Noble Eightfold Path includes right understanding, right thought, right speech, right action, right livelihood, right effort, right mindfulness and right concentration. Through these practices, the distortions in our perceptions and thinking become purified and we return to a more clarified and less suffering state.

---

7   Rob Preece, *The Psychology of Buddhist Tantra* (Ithaca, New York: Snow Lion Publications, 2006), 10.

Following the Noble Eightfold Path leads to the gift of freedom from suffering. As a Buddhist follows the Noble Eightfold Path, the confusion, hindrances, and obstacles which are the result of a buildup of negative thoughts and actions are removed. As the negativities are purified, the practitioner of Buddhism enters a more purified and therefore a more beautified and virtuous state. Pema experienced a minor version of this in her own life. On a three-month retreat, she meditated for the better part of most days and she spoke very little. After this retreat experience, she felt that she accessed a part of herself that was gentle. At the time, she did not experience many negative thoughts, conflicts, or intense feelings. She felt that people could be safer with her and that this gentility made her stronger. This strength enables her to be a compassionate presence for others.

Buddhist practitioners may arrive at a specific awareness that all beings are suffering combined with a desire to help end that suffering. At that time, they may wish to further cultivate a special attitude that all beings are equally valuable and deserve happiness and healing, and then combine that understanding with the sense, "May I be / become the one capable of helping them." Furthermore, like an oncologist whose beloved parent develops a rare form of cancer, a Buddhist practitioner may also cultivate a special type of dedication to their spiritual path, hoping to more quickly find a "cure," or an end to suffering, before losing another beloved being.

This motivation to accelerate one's practice in order to become free from afflictions and develop the capacity to more deeply help others is an important aspect of the tradition to which Pema belongs. In most Buddhist traditions, the Buddha is not a savior. A Buddhist practitioner must be motivated to do their own work. Tibetan Buddhism combines the basic work of removing obstacles and developing virtues in order to heal confusion, a special motivation to help others, *and a deeply energetic and transformative process.*

GETTING STARTED WITH THE PRACTICE
(Amber)

"Pray without ceasing," is how I, Amber, would describe my prayer life. In my early years, I would get up, pray, read scripture, and journal. My journaling included prayers, insights gleaned through reading, and recording daily life experiences. As I grew older, I found these practices plateaued in their ability to transform my heart. I was looking for something but did not know where to search. Then, my sister invited me to a yoga class. I enjoyed the yoga class and became involved in the yoga community. This yoga community introduced me to meditation. I have been practicing yoga and meditation daily for ten years now. I observe that I am at my best when I begin my day with these practices.

Our projects began with light research. Pema guided my reading selections. The practice Pema shared with me was unlike any meditation I experienced previously. What I learned is that research on the specific purification and increase practice does not exist because it is a meditation that is handed down orally from teacher to student. Therefore, Pema suggested that I read about Tibetan Buddhism. I also read a book by Thich Nhat Hanh, a Vietnamese Buddhist author who relies on a compassionate orientation shared with the Vajrayana tradition. Lastly, I chose to read a book on purification practices in various religious traditions. At the same time, Pema read my essay on Christianity from our 2019 World Religions Class, selections from my blog, doctoral thesis project, and my project summary for the practice we shared.

From my research, I learned a few key things that are of particular interest to this practice. Tibetan Buddhism's motivation is healing and transformation of one's own mind – and some Christians might say 'spirit' – in order to be of benefit to all sentient beings. The purpose of this practice is for purification; to remove mental, emotional, or spiritual blockages and obstacles that through confusion have unintentionally accumulated. After purifying blockages, one becomes clean and light so that ultimately you can offer your best self to the world. Rob Preece writes that if we purify "this innate primordial nature, the Buddha nature will manifest spontaneously."[8] Lama Yeshe further explains, "The Buddhist teachings in general and the tantric experience in particular stress that there is a limitless resource of profound wisdom and great lovingkindness within each one of us already. What is necessary is that we tap this resource and activate this potential energy for enlightenment."[9]

Pema and I met to discuss my experience and research with the purification and increase practice on zoom throughout the semester. I began the semester practicing with the original words of taking refuge in the Buddha, Dharma, and Sangha. I realized that my initial connection with the practice was because it felt akin to my practice of yoga. I tentatively shared this thought with Pema and she responded, "That is an interesting insight because this type of practice has been called Yoga of the mind."

My initial thoughts on the purpose of the practice for Christians could be described as a daily baptism. Christians say, "In baptism, you are buried with Christ and you rise out of the baptismal waters to walk in newness of life." Baptism is a ritual where we identify ourselves as a disciple of Christ, but in essence it is a purification practice where we cleanse ourselves from our old ways of thinking, speaking, seeing, hearing, and behaving so that we can embrace our new way, the way of Jesus. This practice goes deeper than a one-time ritual because it is a daily baptism cleansing from the inside out. It is a way of connecting with and reminding ourselves that we are created in the image of God.

---

8 Ibid, 157.
9 Lama Yeshe, *Introduction to Tantra*, 103.

THE MEDITATION

(Pema)

I, Pema, believe it is helpful to understand there is a lack of a standard definition when it comes to meditation. Alexander Berzin, a popular teacher of Tibetan Buddhism, describes meditation as "to habituate ourselves," noting that the Tibetan word for meditation connotes a "beneficial habit" and the Sanskrit word for meditation connotes "to make something happen."[10] He eventually arrives at and shares a definition of "The repeated practice of generating and focusing on a beneficial state of mind to build it up as a habit."[11] According to neuroscientists specializing in the study of meditation and consciousness, "Meditation can be conceptualized as a family of complex emotional and attentional regulatory training regimes developed for various ends, including the cultivation of well-being and emotional balance."[12] Meditation can be of many styles and comes from many traditions, such as Secular Mindfulness, Loving-Kindness Meditation, Hindu Bhakti, Tibetan Buddhism, Jewish Kabbalah, Christian Hesychasm, Zen, Transcendental Meditation, and Kundalini Yoga.[13] Until recently, much of the meditation research did not consider that those different meditations may not have common goals or outcomes or involve the same cognitive mechanisms, but instead simply lumped all types of meditation together.[14] However, more recent studies suggest that "Different mental techniques and meditation practices produce

10 Alexander Berzin. "Main Features of Meditation." *Study Buddhism.* Berzin Archives, September 2011. https://studybuddhism.com/en/tibetan-buddhism/about-buddhism/how-to-study-buddhism/meditation-main-points/main-features-of-meditation.

11 Stefan Schmidt and Harald Walach, "Schmidt S. (2014) Opening Up Meditation for Science: The Development of a Meditation Classification System.," in *Meditation - Neuroscientific Approaches and Philosophical Implications* (Cham: Springer International Publishing, 2014).

12 Antoine Lutz et al., "Attention Regulation and Monitoring in Meditation," Trends in Cognitive Sciences 12, no. 4 (2008): pp. 163-169. pp 163.

13 Daniel Goleman and Ram Dass. *The Meditative Mind: the Varieties of Meditative Experience.* New York: A Jeremy P. Tarcher/Putman Book, published by G.P. Putnams Sons, 2004. pp vii-viii.

14 Daniel Goleman and Richard J. Davidson. *Altered Traits…*

different physiological effects."[15] The wide variety of meditations, from focusing your attention on the breath, to affectively generating and radiating, to the purification and increase, makes it difficult to describe the common threads of meditation (and this difficulty has additional implications for the exploratory research study discussed in the second half of this paper).

We might use psychotherapy as an analogy to better understand the variety of meditation approaches in Buddhism. Some practices are very Cognitive-Behavioral and deal with how to change behaviors and conscious thinking in order to remove obstacles. There is also a foundational Humanistic value of cultivating positive regard for all beings. Some practices could be considered more Psychodynamic, addressing the healing of what some Buddhists may acknowledge as multiple levels of mindlocated starting at the subconscious mind and deeper. Because healing the subconscious can be powerfully transformative in a short period of time, practices at this level are often described as operating like potent "medicine," and require oversight of a "physician," or teacher, in order to be learned and practiced properly. Because of this, some practices are held very privately, and discussed only with the teacher who is guiding the practitioner. While some of the practices which might heal the subconscious are accessible without supervision of a guide, it is still recommended to have one.

Like the approach to many of the meditations within my tradition, the Purification and Increase Refuge Practice is taught orally from teacher to student. Therefore, there is little if no documentation on the practice itself. I will therefore describe the practice in my own words, as I learned it from my teacher in several workshops.[16]

---

15 Hankey, Alex. "Studies of Advanced Stages of Meditation in the Tibetan Buddhist and Vedic Traditions. I: A Comparison of General Changes." *Evidence-Based Complementary and Alternative Medicine* 3, no. 4 (2006): pp 515 and 519.

16 Domo Geshe Rinpoche. Lecture. *Coming Clean: A Spiritual Journey to Wellness*. Presented at Joyful Path Meditation and Healing Center, October 6, 2019; Domo Geshe Rinpoche. Lecture. *Purification and Increase Meditation*. Presented at WCDC Winter Retreat, January 7, 2015. Domo Geshe Rinpoche. Lecture. *Purification and Increase Workshop*. Presented on Zoom, February 20, 2021.

The meditation involves physical movement, repetition, and visualization, all happening simultaneously. The standard practice is three "rounds" on the mala, counting by physically moving one bead at a time on a circular strand of 108 prayer beads until one arrives at the final bead on the strand. The meditation also involves vocalization and the use of repeated phrases. During the first round, as one moves each bead, one says a refuge statement involving the concept of safe direction in the Buddha (Awakened Teacher). There is a component of visualizing purifying light in a specific way, and later visualizing blessing. The second round involves the Dharma (Living Teachings), and the third involves the Sangha (Community of Accomplished "Saints"). The visualizations continue in all rounds. An affective component is also typically part of the meditation in that a sense of safety and trust is generated for a period of time. Practicing this meditation while visualizing the Buddha, Dharma, and Sangha is the Buddhist version of the practice. As part of the case study, Amber also visualized God (El Roi), Jesus, and the Holy Spirit. Visualizing God (El Roi), Jesus, and the Holy Spirit is what we refer to as the Christian version of the practice.

Amber had a surprising number of experiences, many of which might be categorized as life-changing. I have organized quite a number of her experiences into sections on Spiritual Experiences, Healing of Fear and Intimacy (Mental/Emotional), Physical Healing, and the Wisdom of Crossing Over. I will discuss these powerful outcomes and then cover the case study conclusions, which became the incentive for conducting the exploratory research study and including both the case and the exploratory research in this project.

SPIRITUAL EXPERIENCES

(Pema)
Amber began to notice new spiritual experiences and changes within the first week. Early on, Amber experienced waking up at night reciting the lines of the practice. The lines would sometimes come to her as she settled for sleep or when she woke up in the morning. This spontaneous arrival of the lines faded at some point, but she continued to feel a heartfelt call to the practice

19

during those times. On the third day, Amber notes she woke up in the morning with the practice calling to her, "Felt a deep urge to study my scriptures especially the gospels." Amber had changes in her dreams and sleep, having more symbolic and vivid dreams. She also reported that the time of rest directly after practice was a time of insight for her, saying, "A couple of times when I was just resting and being, I felt like there were not visions, but different messages. Several times I was like, 'wow, that is something I need to remember or think about ...'"[17] Reflecting on the observations and insights in her journal entries showed the value of journaling with this practice.

Amber also experienced a deepening in her other practices. Most notably, she felt shifts in her Loving-Kindness practice, which were overall more heartfelt and open. Amber noted when she was leading worship, she had a newfound sense of participating in worshipping while she was leading. She also reported an overall sense of her spirituality "going deeper."

HEALING OF FEAR AND INTIMACY

(Pema)

We met twice during Amber's practice time, mainly for Amber to report on her experience. It was also a time for me to answer any questions she may have or, with the guidance of my teacher, to correct any concerning errors. During our first discussion, Amber said that she felt there was a deep healing of fear. In a later interview, she described the fear as not something that arose from ordinary day-to-day interactions but perhaps something she had carried with her for a long time. This healing began as early as her first practice. In her journal from her first-ever solo practice session, she notes, "[I] laid down after the practice and felt light, lifted, floating. I felt safe, truly safe...like a homecoming."[18]

Amber later shared that the most significant benefit of the practice came regarding intimacy, perhaps on both the spiritual and intrapersonal levels, "As the practice has gone on, I am imagining that I find myself opening and allowing, and it is a wonderful

17 Amber Mattingly. Interview.
18 Amber Mattingly. Personal Practice Journal Entry.

20

freeing feeling."[19] What struck me the most was the intimacy she described *within* herself, as if she felt such a deep sense of safety that she could reconnect to her *whole self* and also to something greater. In response, I recalled the ways traumatic events can be disconnecting and shaming, and Amber's statements led me to ponder how the *relational safety* might help some practitioners heal from the more severe effects of trauma.

However, gaining that level of intimacy was not always an easy process for Amber. This was very similar to my own experience as I first learned these practices. I believe spiritual intimacy implies a deep closeness and connection with something that has significant meaning and purpose. We can be overwhelmed and feel vulnerable when we experience a deep connection through spiritual intimacy in a loving healthy way. If unattended, those feelings of vulnerability can turn into fear. Intimacy is "a relationship that validates all components of personal self-worth."[20] When intimacy is lacking, it opens the door for disconnection and loneliness. "Loneliness is a distinct and aversive state in which feelings of sadness and boredom combine with a yearning for meaningful companionship. When loneliness persists over time, it is a risk factor for developing symptoms of depression and anxiety and for general dissatisfaction with life."[21] Psychology researchers have shown the value of intimate relationships. Yet, Owen takes us from the psychological to the spiritual and asserts there is "overwhelming evidence that intimate relationships and attachment processes are strongly related to mental health and well-being." Subsequently, He establishes "parallels with spiritual intimacy, especially with respect to God."[22] There is a lot at stake; we want connection and well-being from intimacy, but we feel vulnerable and fearful when we get it. In this way, healing requires maturity and courage to move through the feelings of vulnerability and fear that can arise.

19 Amber Mattingly. Interview.
20 Henry Stack quoted in Scott D. Owen, "Spiritual Intimacy: a Qualitative Investigation of Relationships with God and Their Association with Well-Being" (dissertation, Brigham Young University, 2004). pp 3.
21 Ibid, pp 4.
22 Ibid, pp 4.

Contemplative researchers have typically examined the per-ceived *benefits* of meditation and ignored other effects that may appear unrelated to health or well-being,[23] so these challenges of intimacy, vulnerability, and fear did not arise in the literature reviewed. In the Buddhist tradition, the mature practitioner understands that spiritual development and healing are sometimes challenging. The practitioner learns how to stay steady and stable as they gain insights. We also understand that there is a range of spir-itual experiences associated with each type of meditation practice and that those experiences are not necessarily positive or negative. Amber also had this attitude toward the practice. In week three, Amber attributed a positive deepening of her Loving-Kindness (LK) practice to the post-meditation effects of the purification and increase practice and felt very vulnerable in the intimacy she expe-rienced. "It was intense. My ability to feel LK was much greater, and my ability to radiate LK was much stronger. Three issues were coming up: 1) trust is hard, 2) letting go is tough, 3) intimacy is too much/ too intense."[24] In response, Amber came back to her grounding and her maturity as an experienced meditator. To explain her attitude, she quoted from Rob Preece, "In this willing-ness to face unconscious habits we also need compassion towards ourselves as we pass through periods of struggle and discomfort in our practice."[25]

Throughout the case study period and after, Amber acknowl-edges that this practice touched her very deeply and so profoundly that she chose not to tell anyone about it after she learned it. To her, it is the kind of practice one wants to keep close to the heart. This was an intuitive understanding of traditional Tibetan Buddhist wisdom that guides its practitioners to keep their spiritual practices and experiences secret or shared only with spiritual guides. While

23 Jared R. Lindahl, Nathan E. Fisher, David J. Cooper, Rochelle K. Rosen, and Willoughby B. Britton. "The Varieties of Contemplative Experience: A Mixed-Methods Study of Meditation-Related Challenges in Western Buddhists." *PLOS ONE* 12, no. 5 (2017). pp 1.

24 Amber Mattingly. Personal Practice Journal Entry.

25 Rob Preece, *The Psychology of Buddhist Tantra*. (Ithaca, NY: Snow Lion, 2006); pp. 14.

quite open within the research context, Amber still otherwise holds the experiences of this practice close to her heart.

PHYSICAL HEALING

(Pema)

While many physical benefits such as lowered blood pressure, improved immune function, and easing chronic pain and inflammation are reported in meditation research studies, neither Amber nor I anticipated her report of physical healing. Amber suffers from a chronic health condition, where some of the symptoms are chronic leg pain and stomachache. She has had this condition for the majority, if not all, of her life. At four weeks, Amber noted she was experiencing lots of leg pain and "the meditation helps."[26] But most remarkably, in the sixth and final week of the study, she states, "[Looking back on the whole experience,] I recognize that I do not have stomach pain anymore. I typically experience stomachache or pain at least five days per week. I feel more at peace internally." This result foreshadows some of the responses in the research study.

I must note here that both Amber and I encourage people in general, and meditators specifically, to always seek the care of licensed medical professionals for any physical or mental health condition. Despite Amber's incredible report on the alleviation of her physical symptoms, we still advise anyone with a physical health condition to be under the care of a licensed medical professional as well as a qualified spiritual mentor.

WISDOM FROM CROSSING OVER

(Pema)

When asked what insights she gained from the Buddhist practice, Amber spoke of the concepts of purification of body, speech, and mind. She discussed her deepening understanding and embodiment of the Buddhist concepts of right speech, right thinking, and right perceiving. She concluded, "You can read about those things, but this is a practice that embodies those words and makes it very experiential."

---

26 Amber Mattingly. Personal Practice Journal Entry.

23

To better understand the context of Amber's statement, Bikkhu Bodhi states, "The essence of the Buddha's teaching can be summed up in two principles: the Four Noble Truths and the Noble Eightfold Path. The first covers the side of doctrine, and the primary response it elicits is understanding; the second covers the side of discipline, in the broadest sense of that word, and the primary response it calls for is practice."[27] The Noble Eightfold path is discussed as the way of the Fourth Noble Truth. The Noble Eightfold Path is comprised of Right View, Right Intention, Right Speech, Right Action, Right Livelihood, Right Mindfulness, Right Concentration, and the Development of Wisdom.[28] The practice of the Noble Eightfold path, "gives rise to vision, gives rise to knowledge, and leads to peace, to discernment, to enlightenment, to Nibbana."[29]

When I asked her what insights she gained regarding Christian spirituality, Amber said, "a deepening of understanding of Jesus as a healer." She also spoke of a time when she was part of a group practicing Christian spirituality in college. She says, "What I can say about [the spiritual practices] now is that the practices were not very heart-full; they were not very focused on healing. It was more intellectual. They did not penetrate, at least my heart…"[30] In week two of her practice, she wrote in her journal, "I felt like this is yoga for the inside of the body – a deeper cleansing and purifying areas that yoga does not touch."[31]

Amber spoke about the similarities of healing and an embodied experience of the living teachings in both practice versions. "I see the real emphasis in other traditions on this developing of compassion for yourself, and in a way that embodies the Christian ideal, so that I can offer compassion to the world." Her experiences with this practice point to a deepening embodied experience of a loving, healing relationship with God. For me, this ties to her

27 Bodhi, *The Noble Eightfold Path*... pp vii.
28 Ibid.
29 Nyanatiloka, *The Word of the Buddha: an Outline of the Buddha in the Words of the Pali Canon*, 11th ed. (Kandy, Ceylon: Buddhist Publication Society, 1968). pp. 28
30 Amber Mattingly. Interview.
31 Amber Mattingly. Personal Practice Journal Entry.

earlier spiritual theology, "Finding God's abundant unconditional love at the center of this inner sanctuary provides a compass to navigate decisions."

A central issue for Amber in her spiritual theology is what needs to be addressed in God's relationship to humans. Broadly, I think it is to *redefine the relational possibilities.* Amber writes, "In the depth of solitude, a leader cultivates a compassionate heart for their own suffering while accepting the gift of God's unconditional love. When self-compassion and God's love meet, the leader's life becomes fertile ground for experiencing solidarity with all humanity." [32] I think Amber sees all beings as potential leaders, so *redefining the relational possibilities* becomes not only with something greater than ourselves but with ourselves and with others. But perhaps the solitude she speaks of is an outer solitude or perhaps quietude. This practice seems to provide Amber the safe container to experience redefining possibilities and connecting to herself and Others. Toward the end of the study journals, Amber also reports a, "deepening inner strength, clarity and feeling more centered/whole."

INSIGHTS

(Pema)

I began the initial experiment of sharing the purification and increase refuge practice with two questions. The first one was, "Could insights from the practices of Buddhism help move modern Christians and clergy to a deeper understanding of spiritual heartfeltness and also a more fully embodied experience of their spirituality?" Amber reported a deepening of heartfeltness within this case study through examples and expressing a deepening sense of her practice. My second question was, "Could the mechanism or method of practice sometimes be effectively separated from the religious context and moved across religions to function as an authentic practice within that tradition?" I think in this case study, the answer is again yes. However, there are solemn considerations for moving any practice across traditions.

---

32 Amber Mattingly. From the Pew to the Mat.

Although I believe we are all of similar nature and interdependent, our experiences of "Otherness" and marginalization are keys to finding our own spiritual center, our own home location, and our understanding of how to love with inclusion. Even though there are important lessons in interdependence and a sense of "oneness" or belonging, I realize that to minimize our stories of Otherness leads us to a myopic and oppressive understanding of God (and of the Buddhist spiritual life). While I might say ultimately there is no "Other," I often come back to explore a reason for this sense of separate identity. Perhaps a sense of separate identity is part of the mechanism of overcoming our fundamental problems with love and connection. Perhaps in the Christian context, as we experience a transformative shift from "Unknown Other" to the "Sacred Other" (who is not really an "other" at all), we learn how to, "come home to God."

AMBER'S EXPERIENCE

(Amber)

When Pema introduced me to the purification and increase meditation, I immediately fell in love with the practice. I started our project using the Buddhist words, "I take refuge in the Buddha, Dharma, and Sangha." My initial response was, "I feel like I have come home." I experienced feelings of comfort and celebration much like a guest of honor who has been traveling feels when they walk through the door of their home and are greeted by a surprise gathering of close friends and family. The practice immediately began to call to me in a way that I had never experienced in any Christian practice. What I mean is that I would wake up in the middle of the night saying the words in my mind or I would go to sleep with the words on my lips. My dreams even became more vivid, frequent, and somewhat more symbolic. This magnetic quality intrigued me and kept me interested in what lies ahead as I continued to observe the effects of the practice.

Within the first week, the comfort and joy I initially felt were matched with confusion and anxiety. I continued to feel drawn to the practice and safe in the movement and direction, but I began to have questions about what it meant that I, as a Christian, was experiencing a profound sense of welcome in a Buddhist practice. In my journal, I wrote, "Where is this leading me? Am I still following Jesus?" These are very real questions and Pema and I took them seriously. I continued to practice and noticed that a couple of things helped me through my confusion and anxiety. First, my yoga practice taught me to observe what I was feeling and thinking. Instead of being carried away by my thoughts, I was able to step back and become curious about my confusion and anxiety. During one of the practices, I felt deeply these words, "There is no fear in love." With a loving connection, I continued to stay open and curious.

Our project involved learning through experience and learning through research. In my reading, I came across two quotes from Rob Preece. Preece indicates that certain forms of mediation do not "attempt to soothe the turmoil of existence with consoling promises of salvation" and writes that the meditator, – "…chooses

27

to confront the bewildering and chaotic forces of fear, aggression, desire, and pride and to work with them in such a way that they are channeled into creative expression, loving relationships, and wisely engaged forms of life."[33] He also wrote," ...the dark aspects of our Shadow will almost certainly be evoked, and it requires great courage, honesty, and humility to face and transform them."[34] These quotes helped ease the tension of my anxiety and confusion knowing that they were a part of the transformational process.

THEOLOGICAL CONNECTIONS

(Amber)

After more deeply understanding the meditation in the Buddhist tradition, Pema encouraged me to replace the Buddhist words with Christian words. I spent considerable time exploring Christian options. I settled on "El Roi," from Hagar's narrative found in Genesis 16:13, "She gave this name to the Lord who spoke to her: 'You are the God who sees me,' for she said, 'I have now seen the One who sees me.'"[35] El Roi means the God who sees and implied in this meaning is that God sees the suffering of God's creation. This practice gave me the gift of seeing more clearly, so I chose the name for God that best embodied this gift. I chose Jesus as the living Word because in John 1:1-3; 14 our sacred text says, "In the beginning was the Word, and the Word was with God, and the Word was God. He was in the beginning with God. All things came into being through him, and without him not one thing came into being....And the Word became flesh and lived among us, and we have seen his glory, the glory as of a father's only son, full of grace and truth." I chose Spirit as a word that embodied the essence of the Sangha as it was the Spirit that birthed the Christian community and the idea of the communion of saints at Pentecost. As I practiced both the Buddhist and Christian versions, I continued to observe other theological connections.

---

33 Rob Preece, *The Psychology of Buddhist Tantra*. (Ithaca, New York: Snow Lion Publications), 2006, xi.

34 Rob Preece, The Psychology of Buddhist Tantra, 14.

35 *Holy Bible: New Revised Standard Version* Kindle Book. (New York: Harper Catholic Bibles, 2011).

The first theme that emerged during my experience of anxiety and confusion was love so I began to explore the power of love over fear. I felt that love guided me to continue to say, "Yes, I choose to continue to practice this meditation." In the gospels, Jesus invited people to come and see. In John's gospel, we read Jesus asking Philip to "follow me." Then, Philip persuades Nathanael to come and see for himself this Jesus who he speaks of. In my mind, I see Jesus extending a hand to Philip and then Philip extending a hand to Nathanael. As I engaged this new practice, I felt a lot of emotions and visualized a lot of blackness within me that the light had a hard time penetrating. Yet, I felt Jesus extend his hand to me saying, "Come and see." The blackness I visualized within myself during the practice, I interpreted as my fear or ignorance that was an obstacle to the light. I was unaware of the many ways that the image of God in me needed to be set free.

If there are obstacles to becoming aware, then we must strive to remove them. The purification and increase practice like my yoga practice brought me more in touch with imago dei, the image of God within each person, and invited me into the transformational process of becoming the likeness of God in this world.

The purification and increase practice also encouraged me to think about the continued experience of incarnation. For many Christians, the incarnation happened at the birth of Jesus, but I have felt more of a connection to Christian mystics like Father Richard Rohr who see incarnation as happening in every person at all times. I began to think about how the practice invited me to see light entering my body, healing the areas of darkness, and filling my entire body with light. I felt a powerful sense of oneness with the Divine. In my understanding, Jesus came to earth to show what it would look like to be in total union with God and that the power to be in total union with God is available to all. The incarnation did not just happen once but is continuing to happen in each of our lives as we align ourselves with Jesus' teaching and follow him in compassionate action.[36] In my experience of Christianity, I have been inspired by Jesus' words and life. I was taught that to follow Jesus was to obey his commands of love, service, and

36 Phillip Novak, *The World's Wisdom: Sacred Texts of the World's Religions* (New York: Harper One, 1994), 270.

sharing the good news with others. Although these practices are wonderful and necessary, they felt very performance based. Until engaging in this form of meditation, I did not know that I was looking for something to transform me from the inside out. I desire to see my actions reflect the love of God and so how I do things matters as much as what I do in my actions. For me, this practice gave me the opportunity to address "how" I can become more like Christ. This practice also reminds me of the story told in Luke 8:43-48 because the meditation offered healing for my chronic pain. I suffer from an autoimmune disorder that can be debilitating. As I practiced the meditation, I would feel relief from the pain. By the end of our six-week project, I noticed a marked decrease in pain and after one year of practice, I no longer experience episodes of debilitating pain. I have always loved the story of the bleeding woman who touches the fringe of Jesus' cloak. Jesus does not know what happened or who touched him, but he recognizes that a healing energy has gone out from him. After practicing this meditation for over a year, I imagine that Jesus was filled with this type of healing light. When the woman who had been bleeding for 12 years touched Jesus' cloak, this healing light was readily available, he felt the power go out from him, and she was immediately healed.

THE RESEARCH STUDY

(Pema)

In reflecting on our project, Amber and I realized that we were formulating questions and ideas for a larger study. This larger study became the focus of my dissertation at CST and Amber agreed to assist as co-researcher. The study included 35 participants 8 of whom were Christians. The participants were asked to attend a training before they began to practice the meditation, which was led by Pema's spiritual mentor. Then, the participants were asked to practice the purification and increase meditation daily without altering their current spiritual practices. The advice was given to experiment with what time of day works best and then to maintain that time of day for the duration of the project. The participants were given a spiritual assessment before beginning the practice and then again at the end of the project. They journaled daily, filled out a mid-point questionnaire, and then they were invited to attend a final gathering when the project concluded.

We were surprised to find there were few differences between the experience of the Christians and Buddhists. Generally, the differences were in whether someone was a beginning meditator with less than 500 lifetime hours of practice (and probably closer to 200) or a more experienced meditator of more than 1,000 lifetime hours of practice. Key findings of the exploratory study for both Christians and Buddhists included participants reporting more feelings of calm, grounding, and centering; physical healing or the alleviation of pain; a theme of more mindful and kinder communication; effects in healing of relationships, sometimes in conjunction with improved sense of connection or more mindful or kind communication; and changes in sleep patterns and dreaming. Participants reported gaining different types of clarity on their experience, explored better strategies and self-discipline for their practices, and reported new levels of awareness. There was also a distinctive theme in finding confidence, faith, or trust in the practice or in higher spiritual processes or entities such as God. Participants reported on sense of purpose, spiritual needs, orienting to spiritual life, as well as additional insights. Of special interest is meditation-induced light and understanding how the various parts of the purification and increase practice play a role in creating the meditation-induced effects noted in the study.

CHRISTIAN PERSPECTIVES

(Amber)

As the larger project began, I observed the Christians' journal entries wondering if they might experience a level of resistance to the practice like I had experienced. Throughout the study, we asked the participants to fill out a daily journal. This way we could make personal contact with a participant to answer any questions that came up, address concerns, and give personal attention to individual experiences of the practice. The Christians in our study generally leaned towards being open to learning practices from another tradition and had experience in various forms of meditation. Having an openness to learn a practice that was translated from the Buddhist tradition and previous experience in meditation, this Christian group experienced a lesser degree of resistance than might be found in Christians who have little experience with meditation and express concern in learning a practice with roots in another religious tradition. The resistance expressed in the journal entries and the solutions the Christian group found can be organized into two categories: relational and biblical.

RELATIONAL

(Amber)

One participant expressed concern early on in the practice. He noticed that his body felt very tense during the meditation. He wrote, "I noticed that my body was resistant to the practice this morning. Physically I was tense and it felt like my body was pushing against the meditation." As he continued the meditation, he became aware that his challenge centered around his Christian image of God and the visualization in the meditation that asks the practitioner to imagine a black lump at the heart center and that light comes in and vaporizes the black lump. He wrote, "I continue to struggle with the third repetition of the practice, the focus on the heart. Many Christian writers argue this is where the kingdom of

God resides within us, and it's very challenging to visualize a lump of something bad exiting from a place where God resides in me. I realized today that my image of God is limited. I have had a hard time visualizing God sending lights and energy to cleanse my body because that isn't who I understand God to be. While I still am not comfortable with a God of energy and light, I realize that has more to do with me and less to do with this practice itself."

Pema responded to him and asked him to consider what it would mean to him if the black clump was that which separates him from God. Although Buddhists do not have the concept of sin, they do have the concept of accumulating negative karma which can make muddy that which hopes to become clear. In this way, it can function similarly to sin. The participant arrived at a similar conclusion and changed his attitude toward the practice. Instead of thinking about God as the light that he visualized, he began to ask God to remove anything that might separate him from God. He expressed the ask as a deep desire in his heart to draw closer to God. He wrote, "In my meditation, I asked God to remove from me that which keeps me separate from God. As I moved through the meditation, my heart wanted to ask that God remove the sin from my heart, so that by the time I ended the meditation my request became to flush and remove the sin from my thoughts, speech, and heart." Then, he added, "This morning I increased my comfort level considerably with the practice. Instead of, as the practice encourages us to do, visualize light entering our body or negative emotions exiting our body, I've turned it into an ask. For example, I now ask God "to completely fill me with purifying light, sweeping out all negative potentials, obscurations, pollution, and blocks, etc." This has greatly increased my comfort level with the practice."

The relational aspect of the practice affected other participants in the Christian group. One participant wrote that this practice enhanced, "a connection with God and awareness of transformation into being a more loving, compassionate person." Another participant mentioned in the midpoint survey that this practice touched a longing that they did not know that they had deep inside. They stated, "That there is a hunger in me for contemplation like this and stillness. I haven't had that regularly in my own spiritual life; I've done a lot of Bible studies and book studies, engaged in daily prayer during various periods, worked with Spiritual Directors, but nothing like this. I've had very powerful experiences sensing the presence of God within the community and with others. This is different and I find that it's responding to a need that I didn't know I had."

Within the relational effects of the practice, two themes emerged that were quite different from the Christian participants' previous experiences of practices found within the Christian tradition. First, the idea of feeling safe with God, Jesus & the Spirit emerged as a new experience. One participant wrote, "I felt gratitude for the safety. Don't recollect Christianity focusing on feeling safe." Yet another participant noted, " I enjoy the focus on the Trinity. I felt the I-Thou relationship with the Godhead, noting a sense of joy and awe that I could be in relationship with the Ground of All Being. I'm still feeling a sense of awe and immense gratitude. (He asked) "Who are we that God is mindful of us?" He stated, "I felt safe in God's presence, nurtured, cared for, loved, appreciated. Like the love of a mother, unconditional." Second, the purification and increase practice encouraged feeling sensations within the body. One participant wrote that she experienced an "intimate sensation in my body and that is not my experience in Christian practices. Christian (practice) is more intellectual and figuring out the message. I wanted to make meaning of it. It's a necessary complement to the heady Christian practices."

A teenager in our study had the least amount of experience with meditation, but she had participated in a six-week Loving Kindness meditation study. This participant has a chronic illness that affects her sleep, energy, and reduces her appetite. During the six weeks of purification and increase meditation, she reported better sleep, a greater sense of calm, and increased appetite. She reported meeting a resistance that she could not explain. She wrote, " I have a mental block towards this practice that I can't explain. I came to this meditation study with an open mind, and I've been sleeping better and feeling hunger more than I ever used to. I also feel calm, quiet, and alert. Nevertheless, I still have to force myself to go through with the practice. It feels long to me, even though it only takes about thirteen minutes. I also have trouble taking the pressure out of my head and into my heart." Although she could not understand the resistance she felt, the relational aspect of the practice uncovered a deep desire to be closer to God. She noted, "I want to get closer to God. I feel like I have wandered. I no longer feel guided. It impacted me a little bit to take safe direction in God, Jesus, and the Spirit, but the connection I would feel in the practice faded immediately after I finished the practice. So, I would like to know how to sustain that feeling of connection."

BIBLICAL

(Amber)
Many of our Christian participants noted a sense of being called back into biblical study. They highlighted that this calling was to draw a biblical connection to their experience of this practice, address concerns about the practice, or to find new understanding in reading their sacred text. The study of the Christian sacred text seemed to enhance the relational aspect of the practice. One participant felt a deep connection between this practice and the practices she participates in during the Christian season of Lent. She wrote that it felt "appropriate in lent to purify and increase." She also noted that the chanting in the meditation reminded her of a Christian practice that uses Psalm 51. She wrote, " (The) chant O Purify Me was going through my head when I woke up, continued off and on during the practice and afterwards." Another participant felt that the practice reminded her of a verse in the bible. She journaled, "… I envisioned each bead as a golden thread that Jesus was threading inside me, in my body, throat, and mind/heart. It reminded me of the verse in the Bible (maybe in a Psalm?) that says that God has "knit each one of us in our mother's womb." It was a feeling of great intimacy with Jesus."

The Christian practitioner who felt the most resistance to the purification and increase meditation explained, "(I felt a) challenge because (this practice uses) different Christian images of God and divine. Light and energy." Before engaging in this practice, he read the Christian sacred text through a certain lens. After the experience in our study, he stated, "I was trying to contain God. Now I looked for images in our sacred text that use these images like light, etc. This has helped me feel more comfortable. My eyes were opened to see these images in my sacred text which I had never really seen before." He expressed that this practice and having new eyes in his reading of the Christian sacred text, "Left me with a more expansive view of God and the Divine."

Summary

(Amber)

At the midpoint of our project, Pema and I gathered with the Christian group to practice together and then explore the ideas that were emerging and questions that needed further exploration. I appreciated that we did not address the Christian connections during the initial workshop we offered. This allowed questions, ideas, and concerns to emerge organically. We addressed a number of questions about Biblical and theological connections with the Christian group. I offered the connections that I was exploring and many of the participants added the examples of the connections they were drawing.

The group asked many questions. The first question that popped up was why we chose to use "I take safe direction in God, Jesus and the Spirit" in place of the Buddhist "I take safe direction in Buddha, Dharma, Sangha." I explained that I spent at least a month exploring various counterpoints to the Buddhist words, but that I arrived at the words for the Trinity.

I felt that Christians' reference points needed to include these three aspects as they are foundational to any Christian experience and the relational aspect to the trinity holds space for difference across Christian denominations as well. God or the ground of all being needed to be our starting place. Then, Jesus is the word of God made flesh so embodies the qualities of the Dharma or living teachings. The spirit is a strong connection to the Sangha as she is the one who gave birth to the church community at Pentecost and so becomes the connection to the Christian church throughout the ages or what some Christian traditions call the communion of saints. Once I explained how I drew connections across religious

36

traditions from the Buddhist words to using the Trinity for the Christian practice, the group recognized the potential in using these words and most of the participants continued using the words of the Trinity in the meditation. What I did not account for was that in offering the three aspects of the Trinity for the Christian group, I was inviting the Christians to explore their relationship to these aspects of the Godhead. As the purification and increase practice is highly relational in its Buddhist form, I am grateful that my intuition led me to bring that foundational aspect across traditions.

The relational aspect to the practice needs further exploration. In our project, we invited deeply devoted Christians who practice various forms of meditation. This group of Christian practitioners already had a relational aspect to their religious tradition and many of them are leaders within their tradition. We wonder if we were to expand the group to include Christians who are loosely connected to their tradition or do not have experience in meditation, would they meet a greater level of resistance to this highly relational practice or will it lead them to a deeper devotion? Without a good foundation within their expressed religious tradition and knowledge about meditation, would the research team be able to guide them through times of resistance? I have concerns that this meditation might be too intense for beginners without preparation in other skill-building practices. Pema and I have discussed that a new student of this form of meditation must necessarily go through the training presented by a qualified spiritual mentor, and that the skills a student learns through Yoga and Loving Kindness meditation might be starting points for a less experienced practitioner. The ideas for healthy spiritual direction along this path need further development.

As Pema mentioned before, we feel a sense of calling to help relieve the suffering in the world. My experience of this powerful meditation is that this is a piece to the puzzle that has been lost or diminished in the Christian tradition. This meditation offers profound insight, connection to wisdom, a greater level of sensitivity in communication, and an embodied experience of cleansing, healing, and being made ready to serve others. In Duane Bidwell's book, *When One Religion Isn't Enough*, he talks about how Christians used to come to religion looking for a sense of belonging, to know what to believe, and to find rules for behavior. Now, Christians are looking for a way to be and become their best self.[37] In our project, many of our participants stated in their intake forms that becoming their best self is a top priority and they hoped that a result of this experience would be transformation. The experienced Tibetan Buddhists in our group describe the desired transformation as progress to becoming awakened in order to benefit all living beings. Christian transformation could be described as moving from awareness of the image of God to expressing the likeness of God through the imitation of Jesus.

Henri Nouwen captured my feelings at the conclusion of this project when he wrote, "I have been doing a lot of digging lately and I know that I am just beginning to see a little stream bubbling up through the dry sand. I have to keep digging because that little stream comes from a huge reservoir beneath the desert of my life... Perhaps all we need to do is remove the dry sand that covers the well."[38] My hope is that Christians will see that sharing practices with the Sacred Other does not diminish their devotion to their faith tradition, but has the potential to expand their view of God. Our people are crying out for ways in which transformation is possible. Let us follow the words of one of our participants and, *"expand our view of God to include forming connections with the Sacred Other."*

37 Duane R. Bidwell, *When One Religion Isn't Enough: The Lives of Spiritually Fluid People* (Boston: Beacon Press, 2018), 43.
38 Henri J. M. Nouwen, *Life of the Beloved: Spiritual Living in a Secular World* (New York: The Crossroad Publishing Company, 2017), 37-38.

CONCLUSION

(Pema)

Looking back on the shared experience in our projects, I, Pema, must attribute much of our deep learning to the evolution in our relationship from the *Unknown Other* to a *Sacred Other*, along with our ability to trust that our own beliefs and morals will not be diminished by exposure to the diverse and sometimes conflicting views of other living beings. When we reflected back on our learning from our last semester, we realized that our learning has been very deep and healing in both of our lives. This is not a theoretical acknowledgment of the value of interfaith relationships, but rather an embodied awareness – a core knowing of the enrichment possible in our lives.

The practice we shared has not otherwise been researched, as it is not among the more secularized options popular in research today. It is generally passed down from teacher to student in an oral tradition. As a practice that is fundamentally relational, it may be more difficult to research. Given its reported benefits in the Buddhist students I know, combined with Amber's experience, we agree that it is still worth studying further. Because there are a wide variety of cognitive mechanisms in meditation, along with a diverse set of possible beneficial outcomes, it is important to identify the key stances within the meditation practice in order to ensure its essence is properly maintained. To that end, we plan to involve a Buddhist master who has more experience disseminating the practice.

A colleague engaged in improving Christian-Muslim relations once told me that in interfaith work people will come together to communicate a message or to dialogue and understand each other better, but the approach seems mainly collegial and rarely stems from or leads to a sense of deep spiritual friendship, or kinship. Yet I have many Christian colleagues who have offered me friendship and a very intimate visit to their spiritual homes as we work in the service of the Sacred Other. Unlike some chaplains who see and respect the Other from the margins, I willingly step into their worlds. I realize that in order to safely navigate this movement, two points are necessary. The first point is very clearly my North Star

39

of Buddhism, always guiding me back to a home I never left. My work with Amber culminated in a key learning initiated with other colleagues – my second navigational point is my home location within the expression of Christianity as I make a visit in service of the "Sacred Other."

The attitude that *studying* other religious or spiritual traditions helps to enhance one's own faith in one's primary tradition is a principle long-held by some of our Dominican colleagues. But taking it one step further, this shared style (and/or mechanism) of *practice* might offer a way of engaging certain Christians and Buddhists together across religious lines, and combined with the practice's potential to affect relationships positively, may allow the artificial borders between us and our "neighbors" to soften.

I am not inclined to be Christian. I am wholeheartedly a Buddhist who respects and encourages Christians on their path. From that sense of safety and belonging, I am willing to step into their world in my role as a chaplain. I feel that same respect and encouragement from Amber, seeing her willingness to briefly take on the lens of Buddhism in our continued exploration. As we collaborate more deeply on efforts to bring clarity to our spiritual questions, Amber and I hope to continue to observe the effects on ourselves and our relationship. Going forward, will Amber and I discover or observe other insights from our effort to collaborate across traditions? We are looking forward to finding those answers as we head into our next round of research.

This brings me back to a quote that appears in Amber's doctoral project, "Strangers—the others whom we suspect, fear, distrust, dismiss, even damn—may be sacred. They may be living examples of holiness that we need to survive, even thrive in a world where violence aims to separate us and mire us all in despair. Strangers become our teachers if we are willing to pay attention."[39] We two strangers certainly found a similarity in our call to help relieve the suffering of all sentient beings, and have responded in our own uniquely spiritual ways with the wish, "and may I be the one to do it." Our motivation guides us to further explore how this shared practice deepens embodied spirituality and heals suffering.

39 Nancy Haught. *Sacred Strangers: What the Bible's Outsiders Can Teach Christians.* Collegeville, Minnesota: Liturgical Press, 2017.

Topical Line Drives

Straight to the point in 44 pages
https://topicallinedrives.com

www.ingramcontent.com/pod-product-compliance
Lightning Source LLC
Chambersburg PA
CBHW011748020426
42331CB00014B/3317